THE NBA FINALS

by Tyler Omoth

CAPSTONE PRESS
a capstone imprint

Capstone Captivate is published by Capstone Press, an imprint of Capstone.
1710 Roe Crest Drive
North Mankato, Minnesota 56003
www.capstonepub.com

Copyright © 2020 by Capstone. All rights reserved. No part of this publication may be reproduced in whole or in part, or stored in a retrieval system, or transmitted in any form or by any means, electronic, mechanical, photocopying, recording, or otherwise, without written permission of the publisher.

Library of Congress Cataloging-in-Publication Data is available on the Library of Congress website.
ISBN 978-1-5435-9195-8 (hardcover)
ISBN 978-1-4966-5784-8 (paperback)
ISBN 978-1-5435-9201-6 (eBook PDF)

Summary:
Discover the legendary players, thrilling games, and long history of the NBA Finals.

Image Credits
Associated Press: 13, The Canadian Press/Frank Gunn, cover, Charles Knoblock, 7, Eric Risberg, 28, Harold P. Matosian, 27, Randy Rasmussen, 23; Dreamstime: Jerry Coli, 14, 15, 24; Newscom: KRT/Nuccio Dinuzzo, 25, MCT/Jim Rassol, 17, Reuters/USA Today Sports, 19, Sports Chrome, 8, USA Today Sports/Kyle Terada, 21, USA Today Sports/Nick Turchiaro, 10, ZUMA Press/Armando Arorizo, 11, ZUMA Press/Edward A. Ornelas, 18, ZUMA Press/Pi/Javier Rojas, 5; Shutterstock: EFKS, 1

Design Elements: Shutterstock

Editorial Credits
Editor: Gena Chester; Designer: Sarah Bennett; Media Researcher: Eric Gohl; Production Specialist: Spencer Rosio

All internet sites appearing in back matter were available and accurate when this book was sent to press.

```
Printed and bound in the USA.
PA99
```

Table of Contents

INTRODUCTION
Kawhi Time 4

CHAPTER 1
History of the NBA Finals 6

CHAPTER 2
Great Teams 12

CHAPTER 3
Hardwood Heroes 22

Glossary 30
Read More 31
Internet Sites 31
Index 32

Glossary terms are **bold** on first use.

INTRODUCTION

Kawhi Time

The Golden State Warriors were clinging to a narrow lead over the Toronto Raptors in Game 5 of the 2019 NBA Finals. The series was tied 2–2. The Warriors led 95–93 with 5:16 left to play on the clock. Then, Toronto forward Kawhi Leonard decided to take over. He mixed great 3-point shots with power drives to the hoop. He scored 10 straight points for the Raptors, putting his team up 103–97. The Raptors would hold on to win the game. They won again in Game 6 to claim the championship.

Fast Fact!
In 2019, Kawhi won his second NBA Finals Most Valuable Player award. He won the award previously in 2014 with the San Antonio Spurs.

Kawhi Leonard in Game 4 of the 2019 NBA Finals.

CHAPTER 1

History of the NBA Finals

The National Basketball **League** was created in 1937. In 1946, the Basketball Association of America started to play. By 1949, the two leagues came together to create the National Basketball Association (NBA).

The new league had 17 teams. At the end of the season there were **playoffs**. Twelve teams made it to the playoffs. After the first round, the six winning teams played in the next round. Then, with three teams left, the two with the worst records played each other. The winner of that game played the team with the best record in the finals. In the first NBA Finals, the Minneapolis Lakers beat the Syracuse Nationals in a six-game series. The Lakers were the first NBA Finals Champions. Their center, George Mikan, was one of the very first superstars of the NBA.

Minneapolis Lakers center George Mikan shoots over a New York defender. Mikan led the Lakers to five championships as the team's star center.

Wilt Chamberlain (right) is considered one of the all-time greatest basketball players. He holds the record for most games with 50 or more points and has a career total of 31,419 points.

The new league struggled at first. Some teams dropped out. Only eight teams remained for the 1954–1955 season. In the 1960s, the NBA added more teams as basketball became more popular.

Towering centers Wilt Chamberlain and Bill Russell and guard Jerry West were top stars in the NBA. Because they played on different teams, they were **rivals**. This made the game more entertaining. During the 1960s, Chamberlain did things no one had done before. He even scored 100 points in a single game.

More and more fans continued to follow pro basketball into the 1970s and beyond. In 1976, the NBA combined with the American Basketball Association (ABA). Four ABA teams joined the NBA, giving it a total of 22 teams.

Fast Fact!
The Boston Celtics have won the NBA Finals 17 times. The Lakers have won it 16 times. No other team has won more than six titles.

Today, the NBA has 30 teams. They are split into the Eastern and Western **conferences**. When the season is over, the top eight teams from each conference go to the playoffs.

Raptors forward Kawhi Leonard drives to the basket against Warriors defender Alfonzo McKinnie. Kawhi scored 34 points in Game 2 of the 2019 NBA Finals.

There are four rounds of playoff games. In rounds one, two, and three, teams within each conference play against each other. Each matchup is a best-of-seven games. This means the first team to win four games moves on to the next round. After three rounds of playoffs, only two teams remain.

The best team from the West faces the best team from the East in the last round, which is called the NBA Finals. The NBA Finals take place every year in May or June.

The Toronto Raptors celebrate their 2019 Finals win. This was the team's first time winning the championship.

CHAPTER 2

Great Teams

Boston Celtics: 1957–1969

Coach Red Auerbach led the Celtics to their first NBA championship in 1957. His team beat the St. Louis Hawks 4–3 in the series.

That year was the start of a historic run. Over the next 13 years the Celtics won 11 NBA titles. From 1959 to 1966, they won the NBA Finals every year.

Point guard Bob Cousy ran the **offense** and passed the ball. Shooting guard Sam Jones was a quick and reliable scorer. Bill Russell was a great defender. The Celtics team had players who could do it all.

Coach Arnold "Red" Auerbach of the Boston Celtics (right) congratulates Bill Russell after the center scored 10,000 career points. Russell was added to the Naismith Memorial Basketball Hall of Fame in 1975.

Chicago Bulls: 1991–1998

In the 1990s, the Chicago Bulls were the most exciting team in basketball. The team had Michael Jordan as its star player. He helped the Bulls surprise Magic Johnson's Lakers by beating them in 1991.

The Bulls went on to win the Finals in 1992 and 1993. Then they did it again from 1996 to 1998. Fans called the repeated wins a "three-peat."

Superstar Michael Jordan was the clear leader of the 1990s Bulls. But the Bulls had another great scorer—Scottie Pippen. Horace Grant and Dennis Rodman also helped with rebounds and **defense**. The 1990s Bulls were one of the most exciting teams to watch in NBA history.

Forward Scottie Pippen helped the Bulls win six NBA championships. Pippen was the 1994 All-Star MVP.

Michael Jordan is one of the greatest basketball players in NBA history. In his career, Jordan appeared in 14 All-Star games and won the Finals MVP award six times.

Fast Fact!

In tenth grade, Michael Jordan tried out for his high school's varsity basketball team but did not make the cut.

Miami Heat: 2011–2014

When LeBron James joined the Miami Heat in 2010, he promised they would win. He was right. James combined with Dwyane Wade and Chris Bosh to form the "Big Three." The Heat had three superstar players on one team.

It didn't take long for the Big Three to get to work. For four years, they ruled the Eastern Conference. They reached the NBA Finals their very first year together. They lost to the Dallas Mavericks, but that was only the beginning.

The Heat won the Finals the next two years in a row. In year four, they made it to the Finals once again but lost to the San Antonio Spurs. It was a great four-year stretch.

Heat's Dwyane Wade shoots over Spurs defense in Game 7 of the 2013 NBA Finals. The Heat beat the Spurs 95–88 to win the championship.

San Antonio Spurs: 1999–2014

In 1999, the San Antonio Spurs took on the personality of their star player, Tim Duncan. Everything they did, they did steadily and quietly.

Spurs guard Manu Ginobili dribbles against Heat defender Ray Allen during Game 3 of the 2014 Finals. The Spurs won the game 111–92.

Spurs forward Tim Duncan celebrates the team's 2014 NBA Finals win. They beat the Heat 104–87 in Game 5.

Head Coach Greg Popovich had a strong group with Duncan, Tony Parker, and Manu Ginobli. The star players formed a winning team.

The Spurs weren't known for one sort of skill. There weren't many flashy moments. They just did everything very well. They played basketball with basic, good skills. In 15 years, they went to the Finals six times and won it five times.

Golden State Warriors: 2015–2019

The Golden State Warriors scored fast and scored a lot. They were led by Stephen Curry, Klay Thompson, and Kevin Durant. Over four seasons, they averaged 115.5 points per game. Their defense was not the best in the league, but it didn't matter. They scored so fast and so often, the other teams simply couldn't keep up.

The Warriors made it to the NBA Finals every year from 2015 to 2019. They won it three out of four times. Each time but the last, they played the Cleveland Cavaliers. In 2018, they **swept** the series in four games. In 2019, they reached the finals for a fifth straight year. They lost to the Toronto Raptors.

Golden State Warriors guard Steph Curry shoots around LeBron James in Game 4 of the 2018 Finals. Curry scored 37 points in Game 4.

CHAPTER 3

Hardwood Heroes

Magic Johnson: Game 6 of 1980 Finals

The Los Angeles Lakers were ready to win the Finals in 1980. They were leading three games to two over the Philadelphia 76ers. But they had a problem. Their center, Kareem Abdul-Jabbar, was injured. He had been leading the team in scoring, rebounds, and blocking.

Rookie Ervin "Magic" Johnson was the Lakers' point guard—but an unusually tall one. He took Abdul-Jabbar's spot on the tipoff. Johnson ended up playing every position during the game. And he played them all well.

Johnson scored 42 points and grabbed 15 rebounds. The Lakers won the game and the Finals to become the NBA Champions. Johnson was named the Finals MVP.

Magic Johnson (center) celebrates with his team at a victory rally in Los Angeles in 1980. The Los Angeles Lakers beat the Philadelphia 76ers in Game 6 to win the NBA Finals. Johnson won the Finals MVP award.

Michael Jordan: Game 5 of 1997 Finals

By 1997, no one doubted Michael Jordan's greatness. It was Game 5 of the Finals. The Bulls played against the Utah Jazz. Jordan was sick with the flu. He was so sick that at times during the game he could barely stand.

Michael Jordan played with the Chicago Bulls for 13 seasons and the Washington Wizards for two seasons.

That didn't stop him from leading his team to victory. Despite being very sick, Jordan scored 38 points, snagged seven rebounds, and had five assists. With less than 30 seconds to go, he nailed a 3-pointer to give the Bulls the lead. They held on to win the game and the championship. It was a heroic effort from one of the NBA's all-time greats.

Despite being sick with the flu, Jordan managed a spectacular game. He was named the 1997 Finals MVP for his efforts.

Bill Russell: Game 7 of 1962 Finals

The Celtics looked to beat the Los Angeles Lakers in the 1962 Finals. But it was a tough battle. It came down to the last game. At the final whistle, the score was 100–100. A tie meant overtime.

The Celtics center, Bill Russell, was a leader the entire game. He played all 53 minutes, including overtime. He scored 30 points in the game and tied his own Finals record by grabbing 44 rebounds.

From tipoff to the final buzzer, Russell was on the court making sure the Celtics would come out the winner. They won 110–107 after the overtime period.

Giving Back

NBA players are stars on the court and off of it. Many of basketball's biggest stars are involved in **charities**. In 2018, Miami Heat guard Dwyane Wade gave $200,000 to a charity that works to end gun violence. The charity is called March for Our Lives. Portland Trailblazers point guard Damian Lillard works with Portland area schools to teach kids to respect others. His created a program called RESPECT. LeBron James opened the I Promise school for at-risk kids in 2018. The NBA gives out an award each year to a player, coach, or athletic trainer who gives the most to his or her community. Lillard won the 2018–2019 award.

Bill Russell (right) scores a hook shot over Los Angeles player Jim Krebs (left).

LeBron James: Game 7 of 2016 Finals

The greatest plays get legendary nicknames. In the 2016 NBA Finals, LeBron James added to that list.

James scored 27 points in the game, which was not remarkable for him. He was averaging 29.7 points per game throughout the Finals. But against the high-scoring Warriors, his dedication to defense showed his will to win.

With two minutes left in the game, LeBron drove to the hoop and missed his shot. The Warriors grabbed the rebound and sped down the court. Warrior Andre Iguodala went up for a layup, but his shot got blocked. Despite missing his shot on the other end, James had chased down Iguodala and leaped high to swat away his shot. "The Block" helped the Cavaliers go on to win the game and the Finals.

LeBron James (left) famously blocks the shot of Golden State Warriors' Andre Iguodala (right). James blocked a total of three shots in the game, helping the Cavaliers win the series.

Glossary

charity (CHAYR-uh-tee)—a group that raises money or collects goods to help people in need

conference (KAHN-fuhr-uhns)—a grouping of sports teams that play against each other within a league

defense (di-FENS)—the team that tries to stop points from being scored

league (LEEG)—a group of sports teams that play against each other

offense (aw-FENSS)—the team that has the ball and is trying to score

playoff (PLAY-awf)—a series of games played after the regular season to decide a championship

rival (RI-vul)—someone with whom you compete

swept (SWEPT)—to have beaten a team in every game of the series

Read More

Flynn, Brendan. *Superstars of the NBA Finals.* Minneapolis, MN: Pop, 2018.

Kortmeier, Todd. *Inside the NBA Finals.* Mankato, MN: Childs World, 2016.

Morey, Allan. *The NBA Finals.* Minneapolis, MN: Bellwether Media, Inc., 2019.

Internet Sites

Jr. NBA and Jr. WNBA
www.nba.com/kids/

Sports Illustrated for Kids
www.sikids.com/basketball

Youth Basketball of America
www.yboa.org

Index

awards, 4, 22, 26

Boston Celtics, 9, 12, 26
    Auerbach, Red, 12
    Cousy, Bob, 12
    Jones, Sam, 12
    Russell, Bill, 12, 26

Chamberlain, Wilt, 9
charities, 26
Chicago Bulls, 14
    Grant, Horace, 14
    Jordan, Michael, 14, 15, 24–25
    Pippen, Scottie, 14
    Rodman, Dennis, 14
Cleveland Cavaliers, 20
    James, LeBron, 26, 29

Dallas Mavericks, 16

Golden State Warriors, 4, 20, 29
    Curry, Stephen, 20
    Durant, Kevin, 20
    Iguodala, Andre, 29
    Thompson, Klay, 20

Lakers, 9
    Los Angeles, 22, 26
        Abdul-Jabbar, Kareem, 22
        Johnson, Magic, 14, 22
    Minneapolis, 6
        Mikan, George, 6

Miami Heat, 16
    Bosh, Chris, 16
    James, LeBron, 16
    Wade, Dwyane, 16, 26

Philadelphia 76ers, 22
playoffs, 6, 10–11
Portland Trailblazers
    Damiam Lillard, 26

Russell, Bill, 9

San Antonio Spurs, 4, 16, 18–19
    Duncan, Tim, 18, 19
    Ginobli, Manu, 19
    Parker, Tony, 19
    Popovich, Greg, 19
Syracuse Nationals, 6

Toronto Raptors, 4, 20
    Leonard, Kawhi, 4

Utah Jazz, 24

West, Jerry, 9